SUTTON POCKET HISTORIES

THE SLAVE TRADE

JAMES WALVIN

SUTTON PUBLISHING

First published in the United Kingdom in 1999 by
Sutton Publishing Limited · Phoenix Mill
Thrupp · Stroud · Gloucestershire · GL5 2BU

British Library Cataloguing in Publication Data
A catalogue record for this book is available from the British
Library.

ISBN 0-7509-2258-3

Cover illustration: The Slavedeck of the Albaroz, Prize to the HMS
'Albatros' by Daniel Henry Meynell (d. 1865). (*National Maritime
Museum, London, UK/Bridgeman Art Library, London/New York*)

ALAN SUTTON™ and SUTTON™ are the
trade marks of Sutton Publishing Limited

Typeset in 11/16 pt Baskerville.
Typesetting and origination by
Sutton Publishing Limited.
Printed in Great Britain by
The Guernsey Press Company Limited,
Guernsey, Channel Islands.

Contents

	List of Dates	vii
	Introduction	ix
1.	Europe, Africa and Slavery	1
2.	Africa and Africans	23
3.	The Americas	47
4.	Attacking Slavery	74
	Conclusion	102
	Further Reading	105
	Index	107

List of Dates

1562–3 Sir John Hawkins' first English Atlantic slave voyage.

1607 English settlement of Jamestown, Virginia.

1625–55 British settle their own Caribbean islands: Barbados, 1625; Jamaica, 1655.

1672 Foundation of Royal African Company to control British slave trade.

1756–63 Seven Years War, concluded by Treaty of Paris, which granted Grenada, Dominica, St Vincent and Tobago to Britain.

1771–2 Somerset case: Lord Mansfield decides that a slave cannot be removed from England against his/her will. Signals end of slavery in England.

1776–83 War of American Independence.

1783 *Zong* case: insurance claim for the loss of 131 slaves thrown from Liverpool slave ship in 1781.

1787 Foundation of the Society for the Abolition of the Slave Trade.

1789 French Revolution: concepts of Rights of Man and equality seriously disturb slave colonies.

1789 Former slave Olaudah Equiano publishes autobiography.

vii

1791	Slave revolt in St Domingue (Haiti).
1792–1815	Revolutionary and then Napoleonic Wars: naval warfare and disruption throughout Atlantic and Caribbean. Concluded by Treaty of Vienna, 1815.
1804	Haitian independence.
1807	Abolition of the slave trade by Britain and USA.
1816	Bussa's rebellion, Barbados.
1819	Establishment of Royal Navy anti-slave trade squadron off West Africa.
1822	Denmark Vesey's revolt, South Carolina.
1823	Slave rebellion, Demerara (Guyana). Founding of Anti-Slavery Committee, London.
1831	Nat Turner's revolt, Virginia.
1831–2	'Baptist War'; slave revolt in Jamaica.
1834	Slavery replaced by apprenticeship in British colonies.
1838	Full freedom granted in British colonies.
1861–5	American Civil War.
1865	Thirteenth Amendment abolishes slavery in USA.
1886	Slavery abolished in Cuba.
1888	Slavery abolished in Brazil.

Introduction

There have been many slave trades, by land and sea, in recorded history. Slaves were shipped from the edges of the Greek and Roman empires to the imperial heartlands. Africans were moved along the caravan routes, crossing the Sahara to the Mediterranean and beyond. Slaves were shipped from East Africa, north along the Nile to Egypt. Others were moved east and north-east, from the coast of East Africa to Arabia and to India. Slave routes criss-crossed Africa itself. But the term 'the slave trade' has come to mean one particular slaving system: the enforced movement of Africans across the Atlantic into the Americas.

If any one slaving system has established itself in the public mind, it is surely the Atlantic slave trade. It is easy to see why. In recent years there has been a growing awareness of the importance of the slave trade. Television series (*Roots*), major novels (*Beloved*), films (*Amistad*) have all served to confirm a growing public interest in the slave trade, an interest periodically fed by newspapers and magazines, by TV and radio discussions, and by public exhibitions. Behind this growing public awareness lies a number of converging forces, above all perhaps the dramatic changes in black society, on both sides of the Atlantic, since 1945. In the USA, in the West Indies and more recently in Britain itself, the descendants of slaves have sought not merely a political and social voice, but demanded a new kind of history: one which speaks to their own collective past.

These demands have, over the past thirty years, been nurtured by the emergence of a remarkable scholarship devoted to the slave trade and slavery. This book seeks to make sense of that vast and proliferating scholarship for the general reader. It also tries to illustrate the importance of the slave trade, both in its own terms and for the development of the modern western world. The significance of the Atlantic slave trade lies not simply in the story of Africa, nor in that of the enslaved Americas, but in the way Western Europe rose to unprecedented power and material well-being on the back of the Atlantic slave system. What follows then is informed by recent historical scholarship, but it addresses issues which are of contemporary social concern. Curiosity about the Atlantic slave trade has come to occupy a peculiar position, at the intersection of public memory and scholarly research. It is not always an easy or comfortable meeting point.

A number of basic points inform this book. First of all the numbers of Africans drawn into the Atlantic slave trade were stunning. Even today, looking back after the unending horrors of the twentieth century, there is something uniquely terrible about the oceanic slave trade which linked together Europe, Africa and the Americas. Often described as 'the triangular trade' we now know that the slave trade had a geographical and economic complexity which defies this simple geometric description. And yet, however complex the fine details, however much modern scholars have refined our understanding of the slave trade (especially the numbers involved), we remain confronted by an overwhelming historical phenomenon. The slave trade also transformed the face of the Americas, peopling key areas (notably the regions settled by Europeans, from Brazil through the West Indies to the Chesapeake) with Africans and their offspring. Until the 1820s the great majority of people who had crossed the Atlantic to settle in the Americas were African – not European. Unlike the Europeans, however, the Africans were shipped as slaves. Much later, the descendants of those slaves were to move on to populate other regions of the Americas and, later still, many were to relocate to Europe (post-1945).

The emergence of slavery in the Americas had profound effects not merely in the Americas, but also in Africa and Europe. The severest, often devastating, consequences were to be found in a myriad societies within Africa itself. Something in the order of 12 million Africans were herded on to the slave ships on the West African coast. About 10.5 million survived the Atlantic crossing. And these figures were *in addition* to whatever losses were sustained in the *internal* African migrations, as slaves were moved from the inland points of enslavement and on to the European traders on the coast. Moreover, the slave trade had massive ramifications on Europe itself. After all, the Atlantic slave trade was conducted by *Europeans* (later also Americans – from the north and south). Africans were shipped primarily in European ships; they were bought and traded for goods imported or transshipped through Europe. The profits of the slave trade flowed back to Europe; in fact all major Western European maritime nations sought, with varying degrees of success, to create a niche for themselves in the slave trade. The prospects, profits and general commercial attractiveness of the slave trade was irresistible to these countries. So Europe was from the first intimately involved with the development of the slave trade and slavery. Indeed, the slave trade was as much European as it was African or American.

The slave trade was not simply an oceanic phenomenon, but formed one element in a prolonged and protracted movement of African peoples, from the moment of enslavement in the interior to the moment, months – sometimes years –

later when they set down roots in the Americas. This trade in human beings involved much more than an oceanic experience, though the slave ships formed perhaps the most traumatic of these. The Atlantic crossing had fundamental repercussions for the nature and development of slave societies across the Americas. For those Africans who survived, the slave ships left their mark on the slaves' physical condition – quite apart from the mental scars we can scarcely begin to imagine or comprehend. Large numbers entered the Americas with sicknesses caused by conditions on board the slave ships. Many (most?) never forgot the hell of those ships. Even among their descendants, the slave trade became a haunted refrain in collective folk memory, periodically revived and recollected by the chroniclers of slave culture.

The slave trade had such profound effects on the shaping of the Atlantic world – on the desolation of Africa, the rise of the Americas and the prospering of Europe – that we tend to take it for granted. Yet the more closely we study the slave trade the more unusual it appears. Why transport millions of

Africans vast distances to labour at producing commodities which the western world had not really used previously, and which remained, for years, luxury items? Slaves cultivated sugar and rum, tobacco and rice (and a range of other tropical and semi-tropical crops). But why use slaves? And why use *African* slaves? Would it not have been cheaper to use European labour (free or indentured)? Or why not use local Indian labour? In fact, both methods were tried and tested with varying degrees of success.

Similarly, if Europeans insisted on using African labour, why not employ that labour in Africa, to cultivate tropical produce and thus avoid the cost of shipping labour across the Atlantic? Moreover, even if Europeans felt obliged to use African labour in the Americas, why did they have to resort to African *slaves*? After all, Europeans developed their American colonies at the very time they were shedding their addiction to unfree labour in Europe itself. Was there something distinctive about European attitudes towards Africans which enabled Europeans readily to accept that here were people ideally suited to the role of slave to white masters? To put it crudely, did Europeans regard Africans as natural slaves? There are answers to all these questions; answers which form the story of the unfolding of the Atlantic slave trade.

This book seeks to address some of the major issues which have attracted a growing army of historians over the past thirty years. Current slave scholarship tends to produce massive studies (often on very small topics). Here we try to do something different: to confront a massive topic in a tiny format. In trying to make sense of the subject for a broad readership I hope I do not traduce the work of historians more concerned with the fine detail of their chosen field. Without their efforts I could not have written this small book.

I have chosen to approach the topic by looking at the major themes which, it seems to me, need to be addressed. But the whole discussion is placed within a broadly chronological framework. Though the book is devoted to *the slave trade* I need perhaps to explain what I mean by that. This is NOT simply the story of the oceanic movement of Africans into the

Americas. Rather, I hope to locate that movement of African peoples in its broader setting: to discuss its European origins and consequences, to describe the ramifications for Africa (though that term is far too generalised for so vast a complexity of different African peoples and regions) and to sketch the results of the slave trade in the Americas. The risks of omission and corner-cutting are, I think, worth taking if what follows can reach a readership traditionally excluded from historical scholarship. And yet, to repeat, without that scholarship I could not have written this book.

ONE

Europe, Africa and Slavery

Long before the European discovery of the
Americas, Europeans had used Africans as slaves.
Trans-Saharan slave routes had ferried black
Africans to the Mediterranean and thence to
mainland Europe. African slaves could be found in
the great trading ports of the Mediterranean –
Barcelona, Seville, Valencia, Genoa, Florence and
Venice. Even more African slaves were scattered
throughout the Muslim Mediterranean, especially in
Moorish Spain. Black Africa, however, was better
known to Europe not for its slaves, but for a range of
other commercial attractions, notably gold. These
attractions were a major factor in European
(primarily Portuguese) determination to develop
maritime links to West Africa in the fifteenth
century. From bases in south-west Portugal, and

using improvements in cartography and navigation, the Portuguese sailed to the islands of Madeira and then the Azores, thence round the 'bulge' of West Africa. Each fresh voyage yielded commodities and trade – and Africans. By the mid-fifteenth century, the Portuguese had begun to develop their own trading posts on the African coast, from where Africans were fed back to the Atlantic islands and to Portugal. By the end of that century the Portuguese had established treaties with various African states for supplies of African slaves, primarily to work in the new sugar plantations established in São Tome.

Sugar was to prove critical in the story of the slave trade. Sugar cane had moved slowly westward from its native home in south-east Asia, and Europeans had made their first effective contact with cane sugar – and sugar plantations – in the Mediterranean. Cane sugar was costly, and remained an exotic item on the tables of the European rich and elite throughout the late Middle Ages. All that was to change with the emergence of the Atlantic economy. The links between sugar cultivation, plantations and African enslaved labour – forged initially on the

2

Atlantic islands – laid the basis for what was to emerge in the Americas. By the early sixteenth century sugar plantations, using African slaves, already thrived in Madeira and the Canaries. Africans were also introduced to labour in the Azores, the Cape Verde islands, and Spain and Portugal. The critical developments, however, took place in São Tome and Principe, close by the African coast and indeed to supplies of African slaves. But maritime links to West Africa were awkward, and ships returning from there to Europe struggled against prevailing winds and currents.

Europeans had *not* ventured to West Africa specifically in search of slaves. Rather, they hoped to develop a profitable trade in various African commodities, but they quickly acquired local habits, initially from Muslim Africans, of buying and selling slaves locally, to and from other Africans, or transporting them further afield, to the islands or to Europe. This process was in place *before* the emergence of demand in the Americas. Led by Portugal (and prompted by its cosmopolitan mercantile and financial community), Europeans had broken out of their old trading systems (concentrated on the Mediterranean), realising that trade and settlement in the wider world offered the prospect of untold prosperity.

Slaves were, initially, just one element in that burgeoning global trade. But the early trade in humanity came at a time when Western Europe was shedding its own traditional forms of bondage. The Portuguese were aided in their growing involvement with African slavery by the early belief in converting Africans to Christianity. Their righteous intentions, though, were swept aside by the predatory violence of slave traders on the coast, keen to secure as many Africans as possible for the growing trade to the Atlantic islands.

There were, of course, religious objections, largely from Catholic voices who disliked the enslavement of men 'as one buys and sells cattle'. But the settlement of Brazil served to confirm the importance of slaves, and hence to silence critics of African slavery. The initial Portuguese developments in Brazil were unpromising; Indian peoples refused to work as expected, drifting away from the European presence, or simply dying out from imported diseases. European incursions into the Americas were quickly followed by the introduction of sugar cane. Columbus took cane for planting on his second voyage in 1493, but sugar failed to take hold in the Spanish Caribbean, largely because the Spaniards were more attracted to the lucrative prospects on the mainland. But in the 1530s and '40s sugar was successfully transplanted to north-eastern Brazil (using skills and experience acquired in the Atlantic islands). The sugar plantations were initially small, and used Indian labour. But by the mid-sixteenth century Africans had begun to replace Indian labour on the plantations. As sugar production expanded – and European demand and taste for sugar increased – Africans came to dominate the Brazilian sugar plantations. The Africans had a greater resistance than the Indians to European ailments and seemed to offer planters and their backers a more reliable return on their investments. Thereafter, and throughout the history of black slavery across the Americas, planters rarely doubted that Africans were a better investment than Indian peoples.

So the system which was to transform the Atlantic world was in place in Brazil by the last years of the sixteenth century. Plantations, created by European settlers and metropolitan backers and suppliers, and worked by Africans who were shipped across the Atlantic as slaves, produced sugar for a lucrative and voracious European (and ultimately global) market. The numbers of slaves involved were small compared to the enslaved armies which followed. In 1570 there were about 2–3,000 African slaves in Brazil; perhaps 10,000 twenty years later and 16,000 by 1600. By then, Brazil was producing 10,000 tons of sugar a year. But these figures were dwarfed in the course of the next half-century. Between roughly 1600 and 1650 some 200,000 Africans were imported into Brazil. In 1629, 350 Brazilian sugar mills were producing about 22,000 tons of sugar. This massive change was aided by a complexity of forces: by the power of the Portuguese assisted by Dutch finance, by changes in sugar technology and by the relatively swift oceanic passage from north-east Brazil to Europe. Portugal boomed on the back of African-grown

Brazilian sugar; some 40 per cent of the Treasury's income was derived from sugar duties.

Portuguese settlers poured across the Atlantic, but they were hugely outnumbered by the number of Africans. By 1630 there were upwards of 60,000 Africans in Brazil, supplied by a growing armada of Portuguese slave traders, now moving between 10,000 and 15,000 Africans a year across the Atlantic, to Brazil and to other European colonies. Around 10,000 Africans a year were shipped from Angola (mainly through Luanda), thanks to a series of ties forged by the Portuguese slave traders on the coast and African states and kingdoms both there and in the interior. Agents and traders pushed the search for Africans ever deeper into the interior. As a general rule, however, Europeans remained on the coast. Not until the late nineteenth century were Europeans able effectively to penetrate into the heart of the continent – largely because of problems of disease.

The Portuguese also supplied increasing numbers of Africans to the Spanish settlements in the Americas. The Spanish invasions of the Caribbean and Central America had heralded disaster for the native peoples. Indian civilisations simply collapsed before the Spaniards, their alien microbes and the (largely unsuccessful) Spanish efforts to enslave them. The dazzling wealth of Central and South America deflected Spanish attention away from agricultural development in the islands. Africans (often skilled, and from the Atlantic islands) had accompanied Spanish explorers and *conquistadores* from the early voyages onwards. With the decline of the Indian populations, Spanish settlers turned increasingly to Africans whose movement across the Atlantic was licensed from 1518 by *asiento* (or slave-trading) agreements. The Spanish church, anxious to protect the declining Indians, tended to overlook the plight of the African slaves. But the initial Spanish sugar plantations (in Cuba, Santo Domingo and Jamaica) suffered from the flight of the Spanish settlers towards the fabled wealth of the mainland. As a result, the numbers of Africans arriving in the Spanish islands were relatively small compared to Brazil; perhaps 36,000, landing between 1555 and 1595.

The early seventeenth century saw a sharp rise in slave imports. Africans were used to construct the physical face of Spanish America, much of which survives today. By 1610 half of Cuba's population of 20,000 were slaves. Imported Africans (and between 1590 and 1640 the bulk passed through Cartagena and Veracruz) provided a major income for the Spanish Crown, and gradually Spanish American settlements were dotted with African slaves. Half the population of Lima in 1636 was black. In 1570 half the population of Mexico City was white, half African. Africans (slave and free) could be found in all corners of the economies and society of Spanish America; from domestics to miners, from sailors to field labourers. The Spanish settlements wanted ever more Africans, but the licensed Portuguese slave traders simply could not keep up with demand. Other European traders were keen to make up the shortfall. By the mid-seventeenth century about one-third of a million Africans had been shipped into Spanish America. Though Spanish slavery never reached the importance of Brazilian or West Indian slavery, the supplies to Spanish America had shaped the development of the Atlantic slave trade, first among the Portuguese, then among other north European slave traders.

The Portuguese had been keen to preserve a monopoly of Atlantic slave trading, though they occasionally licensed others to help them. But demand in the Americas could not be satisfied by such a monopoly. Traders and privateers – often backed by their governments – began to swarm round the slave settlements and the African coastal supply points. Privateers had long attacked the over-extended Spanish lines of imperial communication. Similarly, they began to intrude on the West African coast, seeking supplies of African slaves to sell in the Americas. Initially, their slave trading resembled piratical raids. When John Hawkins, one of England's early slave traders, was knighted he – symbolically – incorporated an African on his crest. By then, the late sixteenth century, English slave traders had made serious inroads into the Portuguese slave trade. But the most serious threat came from the Dutch from the 1590s. Over the next thirty years the Dutch developed a taste for slave trading. The foundation of the Dutch West Indian Company (WIC), the Dutch seizure of northern Brazil in 1630 and the conquest of Elmina in 1637 ensured a major Dutch presence in the Atlantic slave trade. Though Dutch money and ships had long serviced the Atlantic trade, the Dutch now had an American plantation colony of their own (while developing other colonies too, in Africa, South America and south-east Asia). By the mid-seventeenth century the Dutch had become the world's greatest trading nation, their sailors ranging from Brazil to Japan.

Though in the long term the Dutch proved incapable of hanging on to Brazil, they needed more and more Africans. To secure those Africans the Dutch needed suitable bases in West Africa, and they drove the Portuguese from a number of their established forts and trading posts. Between 1630 and 1651 the Dutch transported an average 2,500 Africans each year to Brazil. The Portuguese were still shipping 3–4,000. Despite local political upheavals, the Brazilian sugar industry thrived – on the back of African slavery. But by the mid-seventeenth century, slavery had slipped out of the sugar plantations (perhaps a quarter of all slaves did not work in sugar after 1650), and slaves could be

11

found in a range of other occupations. Slavery had begun to sink its roots deep into Brazilian society. In all this the commercial Dutch, though they had failed as colonists in the Americas, had greatly helped the establishment of other slave colonies via their loans and expertise. They were especially helpful to the English.

By the time the English established themselves as major players in Atlantic slavery some 630,000 Africans had *already* been shipped into the Americas. Compared to subsequent figures, this number seems small. But behind it of course lay immense African misery and suffering. Though late on the scene, the English brought about a quantum leap in Atlantic slavery. Their timing was fortunate. In the 1620s and '30s Spain was trying to resist Dutch attacks on their empire, while Europe itself was ravaged by the Thirty Years War (1618–48). The English had already developed a taste for slave-grown produce, notably tobacco and sugar, which was imported from the colonies of other Europeans. It seemed clear that the best commercial way forward was to acquire colonies of their own. By the time of Elizabeth's death it was clear that the Americas could yield bounty on an unparalleled scale, to the adventurous (and the lucky). Men with capital from the City (large numbers of them MPs) invested in a shoal of speculative colonial ventures, beginning with Bermuda in 1609–12, but the real colonial success was Barbados, founded in 1625 with City and Dutch money.

Boatloads of English smallholders flocked to the island, cultivating tobacco and cotton and aided by indentured labour. Within thirty years, however, the island had switched to sugar, the smallholdings quickly giving way to larger plantations, owned by expansionist planters. The 5,000 landholdings of 1650 had shrunk to 3,000 in 1680, while large plantations increased from 50 to 150. The whole process was made possible by the arrival of ever more Africans. Dutch slave traders provided Africans, via Pernambuco in Brazil. As indentured British servants became too costly (they wanted freedom and land at the end of their indentures), Barbadian settlers turned to Africa for slaves. Between 1640 and 1700 some 134,000 Africans were imported into Barbados. The Africans came courtesy of the Royal African

Company (founded in 1672 to secure a British monopoly in Atlantic slave trading). In 1655 the black:white population was more or less evenly balanced; by 1680 blacks formed about 70 per cent of the population. Large numbers of whites had moved on, to North America and to Jamaica. Barbadian slave-grown produce had helped to transform the tastes of the British people. Barbados seemed a cornucopia of colonial well-being, though not for the slaves who, as their numerical dominance grew, found themselves controlled by increasingly harsh laws and a punitive legal system. Barbados became a highly segregated society – a model for future slave societies.

The English added to the West Indian possessions with the seizure of Jamaica from the Spanish in 1655, by troops and settlers mainly from Barbados. They quickly followed the Barbados model. Within fifty years blacks had outnumbered whites in Jamaica – and the island had shifted towards sugar plantations. In 1673 of the 17,000 people in Jamaica, 9,500 were black slaves. By 1700 the white population had fallen to 2,000, rising again in the early eighteenth century. In 1740 there were 10,000 whites, but they were surrounded by a sea of 100,000 slaves, the bulk of them toiling on the island's 400 sugar plantations.

Everywhere the pattern was the same. Early settlers struggled to find the right formula: the right export crop, the right landholding and the right form of labour. The West Indians had all initially tried tobacco, but that was swiftly demoted by the explosive growth of the new colonies to the north in the Chesapeake. The colonies in Virginia and Maryland were founded with English money and royal backing, but survived their early years thanks largely to local Indian help. They turned to an Indian crop – tobacco – worked initially by poor white settlers and indentured labourers on smallholdings; between 1630 and 1680, 75,000 whites had settled in the region. But from the 1680s onwards the small planters began to give way to larger plantations, and white labour was replaced by enslaved Africans. Though Africans first landed in Jamestown in 1619, in 1660 there were only 1,700 blacks throughout the Chesapeake, rising to 4,000 in

1680 (most arriving via the Caribbean). In the course of the eighteenth century, however, about 100,000 Africans were imported.

By the end of the eighteenth century the British had important colonies in the Americas. Their sugar islands of Barbados and Jamaica (plus a string of small islands) and the tobacco colonies of Maryland and Virginia had, after a shaky start and failed social–agricultural experiments, proved successful beyond their wildest expectations. The pioneering days had been painful and miserable. But the triumph of local export crops, including cocoa, coffee, indigo and cotton, confirmed the commercial success of slave plantations. As profits flowed back to London (and the slave-trading ports of Bristol and later Liverpool), as the elite planters emerged into a plantocracy of stunning wealth, African slavery had proved itself the critical variable in settlement in the tropical and semi-tropical Americas. Awash with this colonial success and bounty, few contemporary Britons (or other Europeans) stopped to ask what was the cost to the slaves – and to Africa?

In the process of establishing their seventeenth-century slave colonies, the British also secured their position as the emergent, and later the dominant, slave trader in the Atlantic. Between 1660 (when the restored monarchy enthusiastically furthered slave trading) and 1700 the British shipped something like one-third of a million Africans. In the same period the Portuguese – once the dominant trader – shipped 263,700 Africans. The British were in the slave-trading ascendancy, thanks to the establishment of their own booming slave colonies in the West Indies and North America. Initially (and for a long time), however, it was not clear that *slavery* would yield such success. In all those colonies which became slave societies, pioneering settlers did not intend to create slave-based economies. All tried other social and economic arrangements in the early years: free labour, indentured labour, white and Indian labour, sometimes mixed with a few African slaves. There was no sharp distinction, in the years of settlement, between what sort of work should be done by whites, blacks or Indians. Labour was not demarcated by racial divides. But the coming of

17

large numbers of African slaves transformed that equation. There were winners in this process: British finance and British settlers, British cities and ports, and British economic operations. No one could deny that the losers were the cargoes of anonymous Africans whose miseries went unnoticed by their European tormentors.

Slavery existed in all British colonies from the earliest days. But it was not a defining institution. For more than a century before the British settled their slave colonies and emerged as the main Atlantic slave trader, African slaves had been used as chattel slaves in the Atlantic islands and in Brazil. Moreover, slaves were used for all sorts of labour, and where they formed a small percentage of the overall population they tended to be granted a range of social freedoms which were denied slaves in later years. The introduction of sugar transformed everything. In the British case, this was initiated by Barbados.

Though established in Barbados in the 1630s, sugar became really important there in the 1640s (when war raged in Brazil between the Dutch and the Portuguese). Unable to obtain sugar from their traditional sources, the Dutch turned to Barbados. Dutch money, expertise and shipping transformed the island, but thanks to the help of imported African slaves. In 1651 Barbados shipped 3,750 tons of sugar to England, increasing to 9,525 tons in 1669 and to 15,000 tons in the 1670s. Barbados became the most prosperous island on earth – because of the Africans. In the course of the eighteenth century, however, it was displaced by Jamaica. By 1776 Jamaica had 775 plantations and more than 200,000 slaves. This created a sugar revenue of £1.6 million a year. The volumes of slave-grown sugars descending on British ports was staggering. From a few thousand tons in the 1650s, the figure stood at 23,000 in 1700. A century later it was 245,000 tons. The British – and Europeans in general – had become addicted to sweetened foods and drinks. What, after all, could be more British than a sweet cup of tea (the tea imported from China, the sugar from the West Indies and cultivated by slaves shipped across the Atlantic)?

These simple facts are reflections of much broader changes. First, European power and trade had become global. Led by the Spanish and

Portuguese, but consolidated by the Dutch and then the British, Europe had, post-Columbus, rapidly developed oceanic trading links and distant colonies or trading posts on a global scale. By the early seventeenth century British mercantile and political groups (supported at Court) were keen to follow. That involved securing a position within the Atlantic slaving system, the nub of contemporary prosperity. Though the location of colonial wealth was, in this case, in the Americas and though the critical source of labour came from Africa, the commercial – and ideological – impulse behind the whole scheme lay in Europe. The Americas seemed, to many Britons in the early and mid-seventeenth century, to offer solutions to domestic woes; they could solve poverty and overpopulation, and spawn prosperity which would flow back across the Atlantic. Though New England attracted the early colonising efforts, Britons began to gravitate towards the southern colonies. By 1640 52,000 Britons had settled in the sugar and tobacco colonies compared to 22,500 in New England. The numbers heading for the six British colonies in the West Indies were astonishing

– upwards of 225,000 in the period 1610–60. They were backed by interests in London: men with mercantile and shipping experience in older European, African, Asian and American trades. In their turn the colonists received consistent political and state support for these foreign ventures. There were risks throughout; risks to life and limb for the migrants, risks of war, storm and disruption for the investors, and strategic problems for the royal statesmen. But the explosion in tobacco-based wealth confirmed the basic instincts; that there, in the Americas, lay bounty for all – save of course for the Africans.

The colonies in the Americas needed an oceanic lifeline, both for their imports of African labour and for the foodstuffs and material goods they relied on. There thus emerged a new commercial breed: Atlantic traders and shippers, familiar with the social and commercial cultures of West Africa, the West Indies and North America, shipping goods (and peoples) back and forth, on credit, returning with slave-grown produce to repay their British backers. From the mid-seventeenth century, the whole edifice of Atlantic trading was secured by a string of

Navigation Acts, designed to enhance British trade and well-being by the exclusion of others (notably the Dutch, and later the French). Enforced by the Vice-Admiralty Courts, this 'mercantilist system' hinged on the primacy of British interests. It would create much friction with North Americans by the late eighteenth century. Increasingly, the centre-piece of that Atlantic trade was the flow of Africans from West Africa to the slave baracoons of the Caribbean and the Chesapeake (later South Carolina and Georgia). To secure the system against interlopers, the Royal Navy patrolled the slave routes. Generations of Britain's naval heroes from Nelson downwards learned their seamanship in and around the slave routes of the West Indies. Commercial interests, colonial settlement and British state power all came together from the late seventeenth century onwards – and the lynchpin of the entire system was the African slave.

But where did they come from, these armies of Africans whose enslavement and misery – largely hidden from European gaze – was the source of such material bounty and pleasure to the wider world?

TWO

Africa and Africans

British monopoly companies started trading to Africa in 1663, securing a string of posts and forts from Senegambia to Benin. Re-formed as the Royal African Company in 1672, the company attracted London money. Demand for Africans in the Americas was booming and company ships (and others they had hired) ferried vast numbers of Africans into bondage, mainly to Barbados and Jamaica. By the time the monopoly ended in 1712 the company had shipped 120,000 slaves in 500 ships. But even these numbers were not enough to satisfy the planters. Interlopers easily picked their way through the company's defences and by 1700 most slaves arriving in British colonies came by that route. In London – and the colonies – the monopoly in slave trading was denounced ever more sharply.

The objection was on economic grounds (i.e. not enough Africans were being transported). Few objected to the slave trade itself or disputed its morality. British merchants and traders were anxious to take their share of this lucrative trade.

By the mid-seventeenth century London was replacing Amsterdam as the nub of the Atlantic system – its mercantile class, financial systems, shipping and insurance, as well as its physical infrastructure ever more attuned to the peculiarity of the trade to Africa, thence to the Americas with slaves, and back to Britain with slave-grown produce. By 1700 Bristol too had joined in the slaving business, its powerful merchants with their experience in maritime trading anxious to break into the stunning wealth of the Atlantic trade. Slowly Bristol made its presence felt in the slave trade. By 1728–9 half the British tonnage clearing for Africa came from Bristol, and by the 1730s that city had become Britain's biggest slave trader. Ever more Bristol money poured into the trade to Africa, by 1750 amounting to £150,000 a year. But the slave trade had, by mid-century, also begun to attract the attention of Liverpool's merchants.

By the 1730s the British Atlantic slave trade was in full flow. For the rest of that century (and until abolition in 1807) the British became the world's leading slave traders. Between 1700 and 1810 they transported about 3.4 million Africans. Even today, after the horrors of the twentieth century, these remain astonishing figures. They also clearly show how vital the African had become to the British, to merchants and manufacturers at home, to planters in the colonies and to the slave traders whose flotillas of ships kept the whole industry ticking over. The British had not been the first, and they were not alone. But in the course of the eighteenth century, they perfected the Atlantic slave trade, carrying more Africans than anyone else before, and deriving unprecedented well-being from the slave system. The African slave was in effect the human lubricant of a massive Atlantic system.

By the time the British secured their trading position on the West African coast, Europeans had been active there for a century and more. Initially the British were uninterested, allowing the pioneering Portuguese to maintain their claims to a vast stretch of coast. There were of course piratical English raids into the region for slaves and other commodities.

But all that had changed with the foundation of the British West Indian sugar colonies. The British trading presence in West Africa (organised initially as we have seen through monopoly companies) expanded, displacing the Dutch from established positions and creating new ones. Whereas previously they had conducted trade in various commodities, from 1672 onwards the British concentrated on slave trading from their bases in Gambia, Sierra Leone and the Gold Coast. As the trade opened up, as Bristol and Liverpool traders moved in, the numbers of Africans enslaved and transported grew to unprecedented levels. Between 1662 and 1670 something like 6,700 Africans crossed the Atlantic each year in British ships. A century later, the figure had risen to 42,000. The upswing in British slave trading took place in three main periods: 1650–83, 1708–25 and 1746–71. Overall, here was an expansive branch of British maritime trade driven forward to new levels of magnitude and profitability by a more open trade.

A host of British ports rushed to join the lucrative trade in humanity, from Workington to Poole, from Lancaster to Lyme Regis. But the bulk of the trade continued to be dominated by London, Bristol and Liverpool. Until the early eighteenth century, finance from London funded the majority of British slave voyages. But between 1750 and 1780 almost three-quarters of the British slave trade was financed by Liverpool merchants. The City of London, however, remained critical to the Atlantic slave system throughout, its merchants and financiers guaranteeing and remitting bills of exchange used by West Indians, Americans and Liverpudlians. Moreover, they often financed the cargoes of ships from other British ports bound for the slave markets of West Africa.

The object of their commercial (rarely their humane) attention was Africans. The British took African slaves from an enormous stretch of coastline, but their supplies mostly came from more specific locations. The British tended to operate in six major slaving regions on the coast: from Senegambia south to the Gambia river; in Sierra

Leone, the Gold Coast (from the Volta to the Niger), in the Bight of Benin and, further south, from West-Central Africa. At the height of their slave trading power during the eighteenth century the British took most of their slaves from the Bight of Biafra, mainly from among the Igbo peoples of the interior.

It was a trading system which changed over time. As one region faded in importance, supplies of slaves were sought elsewhere. And what dictated these changing trading patterns on the coast were the largely unknown fluctuations in the African hinterlands. Other slaving nations had their own preferred geographical regions of slave trading. But in general, the Europeans vied with each other for the best spots to trade, seeking to secure a commercial and strategic advantage here or there to the disadvantage or exclusion of other European rivals.

The arrival of Africans on the coast was dictated by forces beyond the control of the coast-based Europeans. In places, it is true, agents and emissaries from the trading positions travelled deep into the interior; often these were men of mixed race, established on the coast and able to move more easily inland. Of course the European demand for ever more Africans sent seismic waves throughout the immediate hinterland – and well beyond. The European goods which were traded for slaves, especially firearms (landed in enormous volumes throughout the history of the slave trade), found their way via internal African trading systems deep into societies which had never seen the Europeans or their ships on the coast. But clearly the *awareness* of the European trading presence was disseminated widely. Distant African peoples and states knew that there was a thriving trade in humanity on the coast for which they could secure a number of valued commodities and benefits. Thus, even though they remained well out of sight in their small bases on the coast (or more likely, riding at anchor offshore), slave traders were a known presence to African peoples many miles inland. The European trading presence thus became a corrosive commercial and human virus, spreading its malignancy deep into the interior; it prompted African states and communities to enslave, kidnap or wage war on neighbours and enemies, thus taking the first step in that prolonged

29

and agonising process of moving other Africans down to the coast, thence on to the pestilential slave ships bound for the Americas.

The Europeans had pronounced views of what sort of Africans they wanted for slaves, but the supply of Africans to the coast was dictated by African dealers and middlemen – and by the ebb and flow of conflict in the interior. There were clearly groups of Africans who benefited from supplying slaves. Forms of bondage had existed in Africa before the Europeans' arrival. Indeed the existence of slavery had predisposed Europeans to accept Africans as slaves. The Europeans, however, transformed existing slave systems. The slave ships arrived loaded with a great variety of commodities from Europe and Asia: firearms, alcohol, textiles. All of these stimulated African tastes for imported goods. In return for these – and for other items used as means of exchange (metal bars, cowrie shells from the Maldives) – Africans were enslaved throughout great stretches of the African interior. Warfare and predatory raids between rival states and empires yielded enslaved Africans for transfer on to other

African middlemen and thence, often via tortuous systems of exchange, to the European slave traders. Europeans preferred male slaves, so the slave ships generally carried more men than women (or children).

What the British did was to establish the enslaved basis for colonial wealth, which had profound consequences on both sides of the Atlantic. But which outsiders knew about those consequences unfolding deep in the African interior, far from the eyes of coast-bound Europeans? Some historians feel that the haemorrhage of so many slaves had disastrous consequences for the population of Africa. We know of three major states in West Africa which collapsed in the wake of the slave system (though others rose to power via the same process). Moreover the European presence stimulated slavery *within* Africa, especially of female slaves. It also encouraged an ever more brutal acquisitiveness within African slaving societies.

Most Africans arriving as slaves on the coast had been kidnapped or taken prisoner in warfare or for crimes. They were then normally sold via African (or

Afro-European) middlemen into European hands. In the years of the trading companies, slaves were herded into the slave forts, some of which survive to this day. More common was the loading of Africans on to the slave ships which cruised up and down the coast – or down the larger rivers – searching for slaves to buy. Everywhere, there was protracted haggling between Africans and Europeans; traders and middlemen coaxed each other with gifts and entertainments before agreeing on prices and terms. Thus were Africans finally shifted, from forts, from beaches, from trading posts, coastal baracoons and small boats, on to the Atlantic slave ships. We need to remember, however, that long before most of the African slaves were handed over to the Europeans, they had been slaves in Africa.

The figures – to repeat – are stunning. From the fifteenth to the nineteenth centuries, some 12 million Africans were loaded on to the Atlantic ships; about 10.5 million arrived in the Americas. It was, quite simply, the largest enforced oceanic movement of people ever known. It was, however, a system which was in a constant state of flux. The first

Africans came from coastal regions, and numbers grew dramatically in the course of the seventeenth century. But it was the eighteenth century which saw the massive upswing in transatlantic slave trading. Brazil continued throughout to be a major slave market; so too did the Caribbean. Between 1700 and 1810 more than 6 million Africans (60 per cent of the overall total) crossed the Atlantic. Even after the abolition of the slave trade by the Danes, British and Americans between 1805 and 1808, and despite international agreements against the slave trade, Africans continued to be shipped across the Atlantic in an illicit trade, primarily to the buoyant markets in Cuba and Brazil. More than 2 million Africans were landed in these years.

The Atlantic slave trade involved a host of traders from throughout Europe, Africa and increasingly the Americas. It was a trading system which became ever more efficient. Improvements in shipping and navigation, in cartography and simple maritime experience cut into the initially long periods involved. What had once taken years, by the end of the slave trade, took months. By the nineteenth century slave ships took only three weeks to arrive at Bahia, Brazil. And throughout, few raised their voice in objection. Not until the late eighteenth century did demands begin to be heard for an end to the slave trade; demands which sprang from a changing religious sensibility on both sides of the Atlantic.

Until then, the Atlantic slave trade progressed largely unimpeded. Furthermore, it was pushed forward by critical forces in Europe, Africa and the Americas. There was a shortage of labour in most colonies in the Americas – a shortage which could not be filled by Indians (many of whom died from disease) or migrant European labour (who generally refused to do slave work). It had become clear that African slaves were cheaper than other forms of labour. But it was the *supply* of Africans which proved the critical factor. In those regions of Africa tapped by European traders, slaves could be had in apparent abundance, on conditions which Europeans could manage. And with the development of successful plantations, especially sugar plantations, the Atlantic system simply fell into place. It did so in part thanks to the expansion of

European maritime and financial strength. Europe's Atlantic ports could not resist the temptation to join in the slave trade. But it was the British (with their increasingly efficient shipping system) who, in time, came to dominate the trade, though a substantial number of slave voyages originated in the Americas.

European and American ships converged on their favourite (i.e. most promising) spot or region for slave sales. But the trade on the coast was always a two-way system: a trade between Africans and Europeans/Americans. Because of the lethal disease environment for whites, European traders and ships rarely lingered long on the coast. The longer they stayed, the higher the risks both to the white crews and to the Africans gradually being loaded below decks. As demand for slaves increased, African middlemen and agents increased their demands in prices and goods. In many respects, the European coastal slave traders were at the mercy of their African suppliers.

Slave owners in the Americas generally wanted young African males (who remained the largest single group throughout the history of the Atlantic slave trade). But overall women and children outnumbered men. As the slave trade developed more and more children found their way on to the slave ships. By the time of the 'illicit' nineteenth-century trade, children formed a majority of slaves on the ships. The different regions of Africa yielded very different gender ratios. Some provided many more women than men. Over the entire history of the slave trade, a smaller proportion of women slaves were delivered to the American slave colonies.

Historians have worked hard on the statistics of the slave trade. It seems likely that, overall, something like 13 per cent of all the Africans loaded on to the Atlantic ships died in transit – about 1.5 million in total. Again, levels of mortality tended to improve over time, largely it seems because of the improvements and efficiencies in the shipping process. Quite simply, ships took less time to cross the Atlantic. Moreover the attention paid to slaves seems to have improved, not from any particular sense of humanity, but from simple economic imperatives. The more healthy slaves delivered by the slave traders, the more profitable the venture. Illnesses, deaths and delays meant erosion of the profits. The whole system was an economic structure, designed to yield profitable return to all concerned (except of course the slaves themselves). The figures were worse for slaves from particular regions of Africa, suggesting that much of the problem lay in the transfer from regions within Africa, in addition to time spent on the slave ships. Nonetheless, the level of mortality on the Atlantic slave trade was higher – for black and white – than in other areas of oceanic trade and migration.

Yet it would be wrong to isolate the oceanic experience from what had gone before. Most Africans enslaved and shipped had spent a very long time in transit *in Africa*. It seems likely that the worst mortality rates among enslaved Africans occurred as they moved away from their point of enslavement in the interior to the Europeans' base on the coast. Furthermore large numbers (as many as one-third) of newly arrived Africans died within the first 3–4 years of landfall. The ocean crossing was but one part of a hellish experience for millions of Africans. And though it had its distinctive horrors and terrors – and left severe damage on the physiques and minds of the African survivors – we need to think of the process as a whole; from enslavement within Africa through to survival in the Americas.

Slave captains had to determine the best time to leave the African coast and head into the trade winds for the Americas. The longer they stayed, patrolling up and down the coast in search of a fuller cargo of slaves, the greater the risk to themselves and to the unfortunate Africans already below decks. Even under good commercial conditions, they lingered for months. For the Africans it was the beginning of a new, seaborne nightmare. Prodded, poked, inspected and cleansed, chained together, the Africans – most of whom had never seen a white person before – were then thrust below into the slave decks. The filth and the stench, the irritations of so many terrified people locked together in conditions of stable-like squalor were to characterise life until landfall in the Americas.

Food was taken communally, from small bowls. Lavatories were simply tubs which the slaves had to reach as best they could. Ideally the white crew tried to exercise small groups of slaves daily, but bad weather or shortages of crew (and slave ships were often short-staffed) invariably intervened. On storm-bound crossings, for weeks at a time, the Africans were chained into this fetid, filthy environment. Not surprisingly, stomach ailment – the 'bloody flux' – took hold and wreaked havoc among the slaves, and continued to do so long after the survivors had landed.

The slave ships were generally normal merchant vessels, used for carrying other goods and commodities. After all, many of the ships had already carried full complements of commodities from Britain to West Africa, and they returned to Europe with produce from the Americas: sugar, rum, tobacco and so on. For the transatlantic leg, the crew put in place slatted shelving to fill the holds with as many Africans as possible. The slave ships were medium-sized – on average 100 tons in the British slave trade of the eighteenth century – and were able to leave Africa with cargoes of about 330

African slaves. Invariably, fewer arrived in the
Americas. But by the end of the slave trade, the
ships were bigger and the journey was faster, with a
consequent lowering of oceanic mortality.

Slave ships were highly volatile vessels. Their
human cargoes had to be guarded throughout. If
the crew dropped their guard for a moment they ran
the risk of slave reaction. Africans threw themselves
overboard in desperation; they plotted to free
themselves, to wreak vengeance on the whites, to
escape or take over. About 10 per cent of all slave
voyages experienced some form of slave resistance,
or attacks from the land while still off the coast of
Africa. These ranged from individual acts of
resistance through to utter upheaval which
consumed everyone, black and white, in a cataclysm
of violence. Not surprisingly, slave ships were well
armed, their guns and armaments aimed towards
the enslaved Africans. Africans from certain regions
were notoriously difficult to contain and repress,
possibly because some of them had had military
experience and were prisoners of war who now
found themselves bound for the Americas.

As the vessels pitched their way across the Atlantic – the nature of the voyage of course dependent like all others on the exigencies of the weather – the oceanic miseries of the Africans knew no bounds. The dead were cast overboard, the living remained chained to the dying, sometimes tended by the crew 'doctors' as best they could. We can count the statistics of the voyages – the deaths, illnesses and arrivals. But we will never really know the deep psychic scars affecting those who survived this experience. Significantly, slaves in the Americas remained close to their 'shipmates', survivors of the crossing together. It was this communal suffering which has remained embedded deep in the consciousness of black societies on both sides of the Atlantic.

Landfall brought an end to the ship's torments. But the land had its own tortures. The Africans had been transported to be sold on, again, to new owners in the Americas – owners who expected an economic return on their investment in humanity. As a result they wanted the strongest and healthiest Africans. So the slave captains generally prepared their human cargoes for resale, washing

41

and cleaning, glossing with oil, dyeing grey or white hair, distributing food and tobacco to cheer up the miserable slaves. They often had to dissemble; to make weak or sick slaves look healthier than they were.

But agents and planters in the Americas were themselves accustomed to inspecting newly arrived Africans and were alert to the tricks of the slave captains. They also employed seasoned Africans, slaves accustomed to life ashore who were able to speak to new arrivals, and who reported back on what they found. Sometimes the whole cargo of slaves was prodded onwards, from the slave holds into a nearby baracoon where they were refreshed, fed and treated until they were in a better condition for resale to local slave owners. There were great variations in how the Africans were sold on arrival. Some were already spoken for and were simply handed over to their new owners. But most fell victim to a new round of herding, inspections and sale – often via alarming rushes or stampedes of potential buyers, keen to grab the best (i.e. healthiest) Africans.

The flow of Africans across the Atlantic delivered people from vastly different regions and societies to all the slave societies of the Americas. Though Brazil took most of its slaves from the Bight of Benin and Angola, most other slave societies received Africans from a wide range of African locations. Again, much depended on timing. The twists and turns, the upheavals within Africa, determined which peoples were supplied to the traders on the coast and hence found their way to the American slave plantations. But as demand for African slaves increased, the networks of African enslavement – of violent recruitment of slaves for transfer to Europeans on the coast – grew larger and larger. The end result was that peoples of diverse African societies were swept up in the process of enslavement and transportation. There were, it is true, significant linguistic and cultural groupings among slaves in the Americas – but it was the *diversity* of African slaves and cultures which emerged as the dominant feature. From this African cultural diversity, in conjunction with the dominant local European and American culture, there was shaped the distinctive slave cultures of the Americas. Slaves in the Americas shared a great deal in common. But in time one society differed from another. Slave societies were different in, say, Virginia, Jamaica and Brazil (and there were marked differences among slaves *within* each of those places, depending on the nature of the work they did and the places they lived).

The Atlantic slave trade ferried millions of Africans into permanent bondage in the Americas – a bondage which they bequeathed to their offspring. But it was much more than an oceanic migration of peoples. There had been nothing like it before – or since – in size or in consequence. It produced catastrophic upheavals within Africa, on a scale and across a geographical expanse that historians are only now beginning to unravel. And it enabled Europeans thousands of miles away, in Brazil, the West Indies and North America, to develop land for profitable cultivation.

It is easier, however, to describe this process in broad outline than it is to describe its implications for the

Africans themselves. We need to recall that for those Africans who survived, from enslavement in Africa to the Americas, the process was violent, protracted and punctuated by terrors and fears, and almost certainly by illness. The Africans who stumbled ashore in Brazil, the West Indies or the Chesapeake were sick, cowed and confused. They had spent what must have seemed an eternity, bounced around from one torment to another; from the first moment of violent enslavement, through protracted travel, sale and resale within Africa, sale to the Europeans, the horrors of the Middle Passage, and then the alarms of slave sales in the Americas. Nor did their torments end there. Sale at the dockside or from the American slave baracoon was followed by yet another movement, to a new workplace; normally to a plantation where the labouring gangs needed replenishing by fresh African labour. But newly arrived Africans were anything but fresh. Most were sick and troubled and in no condition or frame of mind to do what was expected of them, i.e. to bend their backs to the task of providing their new owners with a decent return on their investment. Though much depended on what sort of work the slaves did, the general pattern is clear enough. Planters were forced to buy ever more Africans to get the most from their agricultural endeavours. For the newly arrived African, it must have seemed, as they were prodded forward to work in the sugar or tobacco fields, that life's torments would never end.

THREE

The Americas

Until the 1820s the great majority of people crossing the Atlantic to settle in the Americas were Africans. In some regions, notably the sugar-producing regions, Africans and their locally born descendants greatly outnumbered whites (with all the consequent problems of dominance and control for the minority whites). There were of course regions of the Americas where slaves and blacks were rare. But wherever Africans were imported, their prime purpose was to work. The simple rationale for the Atlantic slave trade was to provide labour for European and colonial endeavours which lacked viable alternative forms of labour. But there were enormous variations within slave labour, and though the majority of Africans were destined for plantation labour, even the plantations differed from one crop to another.

In the early years of settlement Africans did not dominate the labour force. Whites, blacks and Indians (and slaves of mixed race) worked alongside each other, and lived cheek by jowl. Work and social arrangements were not segregated by colour or by race. The coming of the plantation, however, put paid to that, replacing them with a highly stratified and segregated labouring order. In time, work came to be divided on racial grounds: only blacks should undertake certain work. The critical change was the development of the sugar plantation, firstly in Brazil, then across the West Indies. By the late sixteenth century there were 150 Spanish plantations in the Americas cultivating 7,500 tons of sugar – thanks to 10,000 slaves. The Portuguese produced ever more sugar on their Brazilian plantations. What had emerged was an apparently perfect formula for sugar production in the Americas: European management and finance, ample suitable American lands – and African labour. The pattern was quickly followed in other areas of European settlement.

The British adopted the system in Barbados. By 1670 there were 900 plantations on that compact island. A similar pattern followed in Jamaica. By the time of American independence (1776), there were perhaps 1,800 sugar plantations in the British West Indies. The plantations transformed the landscape: slaves chopped and burned the natural habitat, planting in its place the crops needed for profitable cultivation. The end result was the gradual transformation of the environment. The appearance of the islands was completely altered from the time when Europeans first settled the region.

Perhaps most striking and memorable were the more splendid plantations and their great houses. Many survive today as tourist attractions. Plantations grew bigger (especially the successful ones), but most were much simpler; crude outposts on the edge of settlement, their labouring black masses kept in place by a blend of cajoling, brute violence and incentives. At the height of Jamaican sugar prosperity, the average size of the local slave labour force was 200 per plantation, managed by a mere handful of whites. The slaves were marshalled into gangs, recruited by strength and ability, the stronger ones undertaking the harsher field work, the weaker ones picking up the trash and generally assisting the ones above them. But sugar was also *processed* on the plantations, and the plantation factories and distilleries required skilled slaves, able to manage the complex process of sugar production. Moreover as the slave societies developed into increasingly sophisticated communities, slaves moved into all areas of the local economy. There were slave artisans – coopers, carpenters, distillers, wheelwrights, builders and the like – all vital to the smooth operation of the plantations. Other slaves were skilled cattlemen, and transport workers, ferrying supplies in and out and moving the sugar to the waiting boats.

There were enslaved sailors throughout the Americas, manning the boats of the inland waterways (especially important in the Chesapeake and the river systems serving the rice plantations of South Carolina). Others worked the coastal waters throughout the Caribbean – it was easier to sail round Jamaica than to cross its mountainous interior. There were slave sailors on the myriad vessels trading north and south between the northern colonies and the Caribbean. Slaves were even used on the transatlantic slave ships. They were used as interpreters, as book-keepers, as domestic servants and nurses, as seamstresses and cooks. In nineteenth-century North America, as the frontier moved westward, large numbers of slaves could be found as cowboys. Indeed there were very few occupations which failed to attract slave skills and efforts, as the slave colonies developed from those raw settlements of frontier days to sophisticated partners in a booming Atlantic economy of the late eighteenth century.

Slave work differed from crop to crop. Sugar was the harshest of taskmasters, largely perhaps because of the physical terrain in which sugar thrived. Much the same was true of rice cultivation in South Carolina (where the land had to be drained and irrigated, and where planting and reaping took place in horrible conditions). Rice plantations developed between 1690 and 1720, again courtesy of new Africans (2,000 a year arriving by the 1730s mainly through Charleston). By 1740, there were about 40,000 slaves in the region. Though the rice was cultivated on plantations, rice slaves worked differently, using a task system which, though sometimes disliked for allowing slaves too much freedom (they were generally freed once their task had been completed), was successful in converting the region to profitable rice cultivation.

The tobacco industry of Virginia and Maryland also came to depend on slaves, though their work was much less onerous than in sugar or rice. Tobacco plantations were relatively small. As late as 1775 about 63 per cent of Virginia's slaves were worked in groups of five. They worked closely with their white owner/overseer. This was a far cry from the huge gangs in the West Indies, marshalled by draconian field discipline. Visitors to the West Indies were often reminded of military images when they first saw the sugar gangs.

Living and working close to white people had enormous consequences for the nature of local slave society. Africans and local-born slaves quickly adopted European (or settler) habits, language for example. Slave women picked up white women's habits (such as shorter periods of breast-feeding, which itself had enormous effects on different slave reproduction habits). The process of slave 'acculturation', then, was very different where black and white worked and lived close together (in the Chesapeake for example) than in the sugar islands, where huge gangs of primarily Africans lived and worked at great distances from local whites. There, they continued to speak their own languages or patois among themselves and to observe their own cultural habits (even in transmuted forms). In brief, they seemed unmistakably *African*. And this was maintained by the regular infusions into their midst of newly arrived Africans from the slave ships. The Chesapeake was able to manage without further African imports from the mid-eighteenth century onwards, thanks to an expanding locally born slave force.

The new Africans brought with them memories of lost African societies, but they also brought illness and distress, much of which was communicated to resident slaves. This continued as long as the Atlantic slave trade thrived and brought Africans across the Atlantic, and helped the memories of Africa to survive in a host of cultural forms. The nightmares of the Atlantic crossing were equally never forgotten.

The plantation was then ubiquitous in the slave societies. But they differed greatly. Some (sugar) were large scale. Others (tobacco and coffee) were small, where black and white worked side by side. On rice and sugar plantations life was harsh in the extreme, the environment or the working regime (or a combination of both) taking its toll of the enslaved labour force. But everywhere it was the imported slaves and their locally born descendants who provided the key to local prosperity.

It was slave labour which generated the wealth so conspicuously displayed by the planters. The fashionable homes in and around Charleston and Savanna, planters' houses bordering the James river in Virginia, the great houses throughout the Caribbean (and even more lavish the homes in Bath and Bristol, whence successful planters retreated when awash with slave-made money) – all and more stood as physical monuments to the slaves' efforts. It was perhaps inevitable that when Americans began the migration westward in the early nineteenth century, they would take with them, into the lands of the mid-West and the Deep South, the plantation, the institution which had already proved itself so effective in the Old South and in the islands. The development of the nineteenth-century US cotton industry was made possible by the rapid creation of yet more slave plantations.

The American cotton frontier had no further need of Africa, however. There was an expanding black population in the eastern states, and American slave traders simply set up shop in eastern cities, or roamed the countryside, buying up slaves for movement westward. The slave trade which characterised the nineteenth-century USA was not transatlantic, but internal; from east to west. The movement in Brazil at the same time was comparable. In the process slave families were broken up and dispersed, adding yet another emotional agony to the litany of miseries visited on the heads of the slaves. Slaves, consigned to new owners, were parted from loved ones and shuffled off, or were put on boats for the river journey down the Ohio or Mississippi, to a new life in the eastern or southern cotton fields. The separation of slaves from their loved ones was the most agonising of scenes, the individual, family and communal cries and wailing recorded time and again clean across the USA and Brazil, from as far north as the streets of Baltimore to the slave depositories of Rio.

In the USA coffles of chained slaves migrating south and west formed a common sight on the early and mid-nineteenth-century roadways and riverboats. We know that about a million slaves crossed state lines in this way between 1810 and 1860. This figure does not include those slaves who were sold *within* the states. Such enforced migrations, clearly different from the oceanic crossings, served to outrage public opinion in the North. The end result was that slavery spread throughout the South. In 1860 there were 380,000 slave owners in the South. And though most owned only small numbers of slaves, the key point to recall is the degree to which slavery had entered the Southern bloodstream. It seemed vital to local well-being. At its best, it afforded great wealth and its impact can still be seen in the spectacular prosperity in New Orleans or Natchez. Here in the American cotton belt was a reprise of an old story: enslaved black misery making possible lavish white material prosperity, reflected in the grandest of mansions built by planters and traders.

Throughout the history of slavery in the Americas the plantation was much more than a place of work. It was also a garrison, an armed and defended outpost in an alien land. This was especially true where planters also found themselves surrounded by alien peoples kept in place by a harsh regime of life and punishment. Indeed the plantation was itself an instrument for the taming of its own labour force. But the plantations of the colonial Americas needed the outside world. They needed the regular supplies from Europe, North America and, of course, from Africa. They needed the equipment and foodstuffs from Britain, the textiles (to clothe the slaves) from India (later from Britain), they required the metalware from the Black Country and Sheffield. Plantations needed the timber and fish from New England. They needed the slaves from Africa. And they required the leatherware and guns from Britain to keep the slaves in their place. In return, the plantations disgorged those tropical and semi-tropical staples which Europe had come to need: sugar and rum, tobacco and coffee, rice (for the starch which shaped eighteenth-century fashionable elegance). Both sides of the Atlantic had become locked into a mutual economic and social interdependence, all of which hinged on the African slaves, shipped into the Americas by the boatload.

In all this, the slave may have seemed out of sight and out of mind. Though small numbers of slaves were deposited in Britain, the great majority laboured in the Americas. Yet the British economy and the British people had become intimately involved with slavery in the Americas. Slave food, clothing, their working instruments (the spades, axes, cutlasses) came from Britain. There were literally hundreds of separate items exported from Britain to the slave colonies. By the time of American independence, the West Indies imported more than £1.5 million-worth of commodities. The slave economies of the Americas formed an important economic engine whose global reach brought enhanced commerce and trade to Britain from all corners of the globe. But within this Atlantic economy the most obvious and enduring of all the imports and exports was the African slave. Bought, bartered, exchanged, inherited, bequeathed – like other forms of trade – the millions of Africans shipped into the Americas were the enslaved lubricant of the whole system. Without them, the system could not have existed, still less thrived, to bring profit and well-being to the metropolis.

The plantations of the Americas also served to *racialise* slavery. Slaves in the Americas were unlike slaves in most previous slave societies, for they were characterised by colour. They were *black* slaves. In the process, it came to be assumed, in the mind of slave owners (later in the conventions of local society, subsequently in law and legal systems), that slave work could *only* be done by black people. Conversely, here was work which white people should not undertake. The slave plantations of the Americas brought into being a new language and mentality of race which was utterly unique and which was to survive the death of slavery itself. Plantations had also proved their worth. They seemed ideally suited to develop lands, and cultivate tropical produce, and were to be transplanted again – long after slavery had ended – clean round the globe.

In slave societies the plantations had been the tool for disciplining Africans to the new regimes of life and labour in an alien environment. But how *did* the slave masters keep so many slaves in place? In the bigger slave communities – where sugar was grown – slaves greatly outnumbered whites. And at harvest time, the slaves were equipped with a fearsome array of tools and weapons – hoes, bills, cutlasses – which could easily have been turned against the white minority (which was so obviously the source of the slaves' ills). Yet, with one spectacular exception (Haiti), slaves did *not* overthrow the system.

Slaves everywhere resisted slavery. They struggled against it, in Africa, on the slave ships and in the Americas. Their resistance took myriad forms and ranged from open physical defiance (for which they were likely to pay a heavy price) through to devious, secretive acts aimed at disrupting the slave owners' will. Slaves also ran away. Sometimes they simply escaped from oppressive circumstances. Often, however, they were running *to* someone: to relatives and loved ones on distant properties. Slave rebellions peppered the history of slavery in the Americas. Sometimes these were violent and destructive, raining death and destruction on whites and their properties. Violent resistance was especially frequent and severe in the West Indian islands – notably in Jamaica. It was less pronounced among North American slaves. Often, the key variable was the presence of Africans, some of whom, enslaved as POWs, may have had military experience in Africa.

Unsuccessful slave rebels, or those merely caught up in plots (or rumours of plots), faced a ghastly fate at the hands of local slave owners and their bloody penal codes. Each slave upheaval invariably prompted a tightening of local slave codes. Slave torture, executions and dismemberment inevitably followed, and surviving slaves were left in no doubt about what would happen to failed resistance. But this was just the most extreme expression of a slave system which always used violence to keep slaves in place. Brutality was the lifeblood of the slave owners' system. Africans were enslaved violently. They were transported through a protracted brutal process. Slave life on the slave ships was an exercise in violence – quite apart from the immiseration of weeks in unspeakable filth and disease. The sales at landfall were, again, characterised by violent experiences. And all this long before the weary Africans were thrust into daily regimes of labour which were themselves orchestrated by threats of violence.

Slaves were kept at work by threats (and the reality) of cuffs, blows, beating and whipping. The bigger slave gangs were supervised by drivers and overseers (big men, slaves themselves) equipped with whips for use on errant slaves. Slave shortcomings (errors, failure to do work properly, poor time-keeping or lack of attention) were dealt with by physical punishment. This was quite apart from the more fearsome treatments doled out for openly truculent behaviour or disobedience; angry words, blows, threats, resistance and running away – all brought punishment on a familiar scale. For those who took the ultimate gamble, threatening or actually harming whites, a ghastly fate was guaranteed. Other slaves saw and remembered the fate of slaves who has tried violent resistance – and failed.

Historians have been unhappy to recount this doleful litany of slave sufferings, not least because it is so easy to sensationalise. But the violence of slave society formed the backcloth against which slaves lived out their lives. Not all slaves suffered in this way, of course. But enough did to ensure that all slaves knew their place, and knew what would happen if they stepped out of line. Of course a bloody penal code existed in England through the years of slavery. But the violence against slaves was not merely a legally sanctioned violence; it formed a key element in daily labouring and social discipline.

Violence alone, however, cannot explain why slavery stayed in place over such a long period of time. After all, slaves had the physical wherewithal to overthrow their tormentors at critical moments. Slaves were cowed by complex forces. Large numbers were ill. As long as the slave trade survived (until 1807) new Africans continued to arrive in the slave colonies, bringing more sick Africans into their midst, though many recovered their strength when they had settled into life in the Americas.

Equally – and this seems curious to modern eyes – large numbers of slaves had incentives *not* to resist too vigorously. For a start, slaves had families and loved ones who could be harmed by the failed resistance of relatives. Slaves, naturally, worried and cared about the well-being of loved ones, and were unwilling to put them in harm's way. Similarly, young, growing slaves were taught the dos and don'ts of slave life; of knowing how far they could or could not go in confronting whites. Slave families and communities – shaped despite the harsh circumstances of local life – were not prepared or willing to jeopardise themselves by careless truculence or violent behaviour. Moreover most slave owners tried to incorporate incentives (small and insignificant as they seem in retrospect) into local slave life and work, and these rewarded application, industry and loyalty.

Across the slave Americas, slave cultures emerged from the survivals of Africa and started to adopt local colonial or European cultures. The process was similar throughout the Americas, but the outcome was different from one colony to another. Africans arrived alone, most of them were sick (many died within the first three years) and with no material possessions. But all were united by the traumatic experience of enslavement and the oceanic crossing. Obviously they also infused into local society a myriad cultural elements from their varied African origins: their facial and body markings, their languages and customs, their beliefs and social organisations.

Slaves tended to gravitate towards other Africans they recognised (easier to do in the eighteenth-century British islands, where 80 per cent of the new slaves were Igbo speakers). Visitors were struck by the way slaves gravitated, in their social hours, to the company of their own 'nation'. But they also had to adapt to local life. They learned the basics of their masters' European language, or a local variant of it. At the very least they had to understand and be understood; ignorance inevitably incurred punishment. Everywhere – from Brazil to the Sea Islands of South Carolina – a local patois developed, from African roots blended with European languages. There was, however, always a need for African linguists, on the African coast, at sea and in the colonies, to mediate between Africans and whites. In time, there evolved a web of Creole languages spanning the whole of the Atlantic world, enabling the peoples of Africa, Europe and the Americas to understand each other.

Across the Americas slaves shaped their own local culture. Everywhere they made music – often encouraged by whites who came to believe in the uniqueness of African musicality, employing black musicians in Europe and the Americas for their own pleasure. Slaves also made their own musical instruments; from bones, skins, gourds, string and calabashes. At every slave holiday or festival – high days, crop-over, New Year, marriage or burials and increasingly at Christian ceremonies – slaves played music and danced. The iconography of slave life is filled with images of slave music-making and dancing. Europeans assumed that the slaves' musicality was a survival of African cultural attachments. They were less keen, however, on slave drumming, believing that drums provided slaves with the means of communicating with each other, especially to plot. Time and again, Europeans described slave social life as *African*.

Whites were most troubled by slave adherence to their African religions, even when blended with elements of Christianity. Slaves' attachment to old gods, spirits, magic and other supernatural forces was attacked by whites everywhere. At a time when Europeans were shedding their own traditional attachment to magic and 'superstitions', they were confronted by slaves who continued to hold them dear. Slave priests and soothsayers, obeah men and women, all and more were seen as threats to white control. Even when slaves were converted to Christianity they had the unnerving habit of transforming their new faith into something altogether more 'African' than Europeans liked; it was loud and declamatory, ecstatic and undisciplined, and often musical. It was an uncomfortable reminder of Africa. Black Christianity often troubled slave owners. The vernacular of the Old Testament, black preachers, black chapels and congregations, all provided slaves with social and ideological alternatives to their owners' world.

There were important links between slave Christianity and black resistance. In North America the Denmark Vesey upheaval in South Carolina (1822) and Nat Turner's rebellion in Virginia (1831) were shaped by slave Christians. And the same was true of the revolts in the West Indies: in Barbados (1816), Demerara (1823) and Jamaica (the 'Baptist War', 1831–2). Slave owners had once worried about their slaves *as Africans*. By the early nineteenth century (the slave trade had been banned in 1807) they worried about them *as Christians*. Around the Bible and the Church there emerged distinct social and cultural rallying points for the converted slaves. It was a perfect illustration of the way the cultures of Africa and Europe blended into something unique in the slave quarters of the Americas.

Even more crucial perhaps was the growth of slave families and communities. Africans arrived alone. And despite the destructiveness of slavery, slaves created for themselves family structures which formed the bedrock of social life. Family networks formed the basis for ties of kinship, friendship and community. Slave communities developed into much more than a mere aggregation of labourers, brought into being by the owners, for their own economic purposes. Sometimes slave family life was hard to create, and it was difficult for it to survive. In pioneering days (men outnumbering women) and when slaves were forcibly removed for sale elsewhere (common in the nineteenth century in the USA), slave families suffered grievously. Yet, despite these and other obstacles the slave family prospered. And it was within the slave family that young slaves learned from parents and grandparents the lessons of how to cope in a hostile and dangerous world. Around the family grouping there emerged the local slave community: huddles of slave homes which developed their own identity and cultural habits. In turn, these shaped the individual and collective slave identity across the Americas (though each had its own characteristics). But slave life and culture could rarely escape the influence of local white society. At its most obvious in language, white society shaped key areas of slave culture.

Slaves also developed skills which were marketable, and which brought enhanced material well-being to the slave home and community. Gradually, large numbers of slaves improved their material surroundings, by their own efforts, in their own time. This was at its most obvious at high days and holidays (especially New Year and *Mardi Gras*) when slaves dressed up in the most elaborate of clothing to enjoy their customary rights. Fancy clothing, jewellery, artefacts in the homes; all and more emerged among people who seem, at first sight, to have had little to show for their efforts – and whose immediate ancestors had stepped from the slave ships naked, sick and with no possessions. Slave culture, then, involved much more than beliefs and ceremonies, for it embraced patterns of work, of living and material acquisition which served to moderate the bitterness of slave life. Slave culture was a lived experience, bequeathed to younger generations.

Slave owners everywhere continued to keep as tight a control over their human wards as possible. Their dominance ranged from the most grotesque of violent regimes – backed by local (and metropolitan) laws – through to a more benign administration. Sensible slave owners came to accept that they got the best from their slaves *not* by oppressing them at every turn. But circumstances varied greatly. Whites thought it hard to manage the large sugar gangs without brute force and a regular regime of blows and threats. Even then, the system was lubricated by incentives and rewards (especially for the elite slaves). Yet even when work was not unduly violent or oppressive, slave truculence was universal. Resistant, sullen and runaway slaves constantly surprised their owners. Slave resistance was a feature of slave society everywhere, ranging from the most deceptive, almost invisible form (sluggish responses, foot-dragging and muttered insults) through to fierce physical reactions, plots and violent aggressiveness. The destructive cataclysm in the French island of St Domingue in the 1790s was unique. But slave owners *feared* the prospects of such slave outbursts. Indeed the fear of slave violence was the permanent nightmare suffered by whites across the enslaved Americas.

The management of slaves (how to keep them at work, how to contain their pleasures and their idle moments, how to channel their social or religious exuberance) taxed slave owners from first to last. The obvious answer was the threat of physical punishment and violence. The lash was rarely out of sight in the major slave societies. But violence alone could not keep the slave system in place. Equally, slaves realised that violence and physical resistance were extremely risky. Hence slaves everywhere resorted to other forms of resistance: craftier strategies which harmed but left no traces. Slaves coped with the pains of slavery as best they could, grudgingly accommodating when they had to, resisting when they could. Sometimes, they were forced into the most desperate of reactions. Often, of course, they paid with their lives for their hostility to their owners and other whites.

Here was a system which, for all its undoubted material benefits to white settlers and to Europe, could be kept in place only by a range of extraordinary harshness. For all the incentives and bonuses, violence, ultimately, was the lubricant of the entire slave system. Yet it was becoming ever more problematic, and by the late eighteenth century there was a growing number of Europeans who worried that a system which was so addicted to persistent brutality was increasingly hard to justify. What justifications could be offered to defend the more outrageous forms of plantocratic violence? Thus, at the very height of its success, slavery in the Americas found itself under attack from critics in Europe.

FOUR

Attacking Slavery

There had been critics of the slave trade from the earliest days, but criticism was drowned by the emergence of slave-based prosperity. Who could doubt the material and financial benefits which flowed back to Europe, and to European settlers in the Americas? To those most actively involved in the slave trade – the shippers and merchants, the manufacturers and planters, the financial backers and importers of slave-grown goods – slavery was a cornucopia which defied criticism. What was the alternative? Free, Indian and indentured labour had all been tried. But nothing had proved so successful, so lucrative and so manageable and accessible as African slavery. Where else but Africa could labour be had in such abundance (and at what seemed such reasonable cost)? The Atlantic slave system created its own economic rationality. It seemed natural, profitable and irreplaceable; the only secure form of labour to feed the voracious demands of the plantations in the Americas. To outsiders, especially Europeans, slavery seemed far removed from their immediate concerns. But who was ultimately responsible for delivering the sugar, rice and tobacco to their tables?

The cost of African slaves increased in the eighteenth century, and some slave colonies were able to cut their dependence on imported Africans. The natural growth of the North American slave population meant that Africans were no longer needed by the end of the eighteenth century. But the sugar colonies (Barbados excepted) still yearned for ever more Africans. It was a vicious circle. The more they bought, the more they required, because a large proportion died soon after landfall. And new developments always required more Africans, most spectacularly St Domingue from the mid-eighteenth century. Yet in the years when the Europeans, especially the British, were loading record levels of Africans into their slave ships, voices were finally being raised against the trade.

The forces which eventually united against the Atlantic slave system emerged from diverse intellectual and religious origins. Among the earliest critics were the Quakers. Their objections to slavery emerged in the late seventeenth century and formed part of their communal response to the persecution of minorities by an over-powerful state. But even Quakers did not always obey the objections of their leader George Fox, and of periodic *Advices*. After all, the Atlantic slave trade provided a growing band of Quaker businessmen with ample opportunities for trade. Quakers in Philadelphia were among the first to object to the slave trade, urging British Quakers to follow suit. They disliked it on theological grounds, but a number of them felt that free trade, rather than slavery, would provide a better (more profitable) way of dealing with Africa. British Quakers began to publish anti-slavery literature from the 1760s and when, in 1787, the formal campaign was launched in London against the slave trade, a majority of the founding members were Quakers.

Other anti-slavery forces were also at work. The American Revolution of 1776, though ultimately ushering in the newly independent United States which embraced slavery, raised issues of equality and citizenship which had implications for the slavery debate. In its turn, the ideals of that revolution had been shaped both by the practicalities of American politics and by more abstract ideas which flowed from the Enlightenment. Once Americans (and others) began to debate the issue of equality, it was but a short step to discussing equality for slaves.

Compounding these theoretical issues were the changes in economic thought, promoted most famously by Adam Smith in *The Wealth of Nations* (1776), which argued for a greater freedom in economic affairs. As we have seen, Atlantic slavery had been forged by restrictions and controls; by efforts to keep others outside the nation-states' self-interests. And, of course, slavery was the polar opposite of free labour. Though the post-1776 economic debates seemed abstract, they converged with a broader ideological debate about rights, forged by the Enlightenment, and by the American Revolution. Within the USA, however, there was, from the first, an obvious friction between debates about freedom and the vitality of local slavery.

Slavery in North America thrived in the early nineteenth century, thanks to the cotton revolution. As the frontier moved westward, so too did slavery, on the cotton plantations of the west and South. Again, Europe was involved. American cotton fuelled the textile revolution in Britain. Indeed the number of slaves in the USA increased dramatically, from 697,897 in 1790 to 3,953,760 in 1860. But these slaves were local-born. The slave trade of the nineteenth-century USA was not African and transatlantic, but local and internal; slaves were bought from the old slaving states in the east (the 'Old South') (often via family break-up) and moved westward on to the buoyant cotton plantations. American objections to slavery tended to be waved aside, again because of the economic importance of cotton. But in precisely these years the British campaign against their own slave system reached its height.

The initial point of attack for British abolition was the slave trade. It was relatively simple to illustrate and publicise the human outrages on the slave ships. There were plenty of people – sailors, traders, merchants and colonials – who had seen those outrages at first hand. But why should such scenes offend in 1787, and not in 1687? In fact times were changing. There was an emergent new sensibility (admittedly a minority affair) about cruelty and inhumanity. This focused on the slave trade. It was a sensibility which was, in part, shaped by the changing face of British nonconformity. The Quakers were at the fore, but in time the abolitionist movement drew upon a very broad range of religious sentiment. Indeed most of the anti-slavery petitions which flowed into Parliament in the last phase of slavery originated in churches and chapels.

The campaign proper against the slave trade was launched in 1787. The thrust of the initial objections were religious and humane: that the slave trade was a monstrous and unchristian business which should be brought to an end. It was, of course, fiercely resisted in Parliament by MPs and the Lords, prompted by the activities and propaganda of the West Indians. To drum up abolitionist information, Thomas Clarkson toured the country, interviewing men involved in the trade, collecting artefacts and accumulating evidence that Africa could yield much more than enslaved humanity. From the first there was an assumption that open trade, in other commodities and goods, would yield a healthy trade in lieu of African slaves. It was a point made by the African abolitionist Olaudah Equiano in his autobiography. But abolitionists faced stiff opposition from planters, merchants and others whose economic well-being was rooted in the Atlantic slave trade. Moreover it had become so massive an industry that many simply could not imagine life without it. The slave trade and its economic consequences reached deep into the heart of British society. Thus, when the attack against the slave trade was first launched in 1787, it seemed hopelessly optimistic. Yet it had succeeded within twenty years. This was not simply because the slave system was no longer economically important. Indeed at the moment the first abolitionist attack was launched, the Atlantic system seemed as secure and buoyant as ever.

Within months the London-based abolitionists had friends and contacts across the face of Britain. Quakers again were critical, for it was the nationwide Quaker network of Friends and sympathisers which came to the assistance of the campaign against the slave trade. There was a ready-made national network of Quakers which provided the organisational framework for abolition activities. This network was especially important for the gathering of local signatures on abolitionist petitions. In these activities, women were active from an early date. Later, they became the foot soldiers of the anti-slavery movement. British women, forced to operate, on the whole, in isolation from their menfolk, made great play of the outrages against African women (and against slave families in general). Their efforts reached directly into British domestic life. Thus, the campaign against the slave trade was also a campaign about gender.

Abolitionists made clever use of graphic material. Images of supplicant slaves in chains, the famous cross-section of a slave ship, illustrating the shocking crowding of slaves between decks, all and more brought home the visual realities of slavery. Lecturers, headed by Thomas Clarkson, wandered the country, alerting large crowds to the same realities and encouraging anti-slave trade petitions. Wilberforce led the parliamentary attack. The result was an astonishing shower of abolition petitions descending on Parliament in the years between 1787 and 1792. To judge by the number of signatures lodged with abolition petitions, within a very short time, it seemed that the nation had turned against the slave trade.

The whole debate about slavery was transformed by the French Revolution in 1789. First, the ideals – of liberty, equality and fraternity – had fundamental repercussions for the debate about slavery. If *all* men were equal, that surely must include black men and women. Initially, the revolution seemed to give a boost to abolition. But when the revolution drifted into violence at home, when the Jacobins pushed the movement into regicidal violence, even stout-hearted British supporters began to shy away from reform in general, incuding abolition. Moreover the revolution prompted massive upheavals in the

French colony of St Domingue which had since the mid-century been the boom island of the Caribbean, its profitable sugar and coffee lands flooded with unprecedented numbers of newly arrived Africans. The revolution played itself out in the Caribbean in a crescendo of sectional and racial violence. The slaves rose and swept everything before them in the most successful and violent of all New World slave revolts. They also destroyed the French army sent to curb them, and then a British army sent to secure the colony for the British. By 1796 St Domingue (Haiti) had become a byword for what might happen if outsiders tampered with the slave system. It was as though the plantocracy's worst predictions had come true. Following the loss of the British invading force (mainly to disease, but also to the superior tactics of the ex-slaves), more and more people asked the question: was it worth it?

The Haitian revolt had a curiously complex result. In the short term it cautioned more and more Britons, already sympathetic to abolition, against the rush to end the slave trade. They looked at events in Haiti with horror and worried that any tampering with the British system might have the same results. After all, this is what planters had always argued: remove the restraints of slavery, and the free slaves would simply revert to their 'natural' African vices. This was of course a racial justification for economic self-interest. But, by the mid-1790s, it had a plausibility to British onlookers. The Haitian revolution established the first black republic outside Africa, and (after the USA) the second post-colonial society in the modern world. It loosened the chains of slavery. British statesmen and politicians, in addition to those actively involved, had begun to ask the question: was it worth it? Was the retention and securing of slave colonies worth the vast cost (the British lost *c.* 40,000 men in the doomed Haitian invasion)? Though this question was rarely expressed in arithmetical or accountancy terms, by the mid-1790s the cost and value of the slave system had become a critical factor in British considerations.

So it was that France and Haiti cast a shadow across the debate about the slave trade in Britain. Though a substantial degree of abolition had been secured in

Parliament by 1792, it proved impossible to secure enough votes in both Houses to bring the system down. Moreover from 1793 the British were at war with France. Yet by the mid-1790s a critical juncture of forces had been secured. The initial cries of outrage against the inhumanity and unchristian nature of the slave trade had now been joined by a rumble of economic dissent. Was slavery becoming less viable? In the event, the first abolition (passed in 1806) was directed against the slave trade to *foreign* and new slave colonies (where most British sales took place). This broke the back of the British slave trading system. The trade was completely outlawed in 1807.

Abolitionist tactics had been brilliantly successful: lectures, nationwide agitation, petitions signed by tens of thousands of people, lobbying of MPs, sugar boycotts – all and more sowed the seeds of popular abolition. But, though the Atlantic slave trade had been outlawed (by the Americans and the Danes as well) slavery in the colonies continued. Abolition left about 600,000 Africans and their descendants toiling as slaves in the West Indies. The British abolitionists' intention was to starve the planters into submission. By denying them fresh supplies of Africans it was hoped that they would treat their existing slaves better, and free labour would emerge as a better alternative to slavery. Events were to prove them wrong. Slave registration (a census of slaves) and information from the growing army of nonconformist missionaries at work in the islands after the Napeolonic Wars showed that the slaves' lot continued to be miserable. This was confirmed by the continuing rumble of slave unrest, and by the regular revolts in the British colonies (1816, 1823 and 1831–2). It seemed clear enough that slavery would not die a natural death, but would have to be given the *coup de grace*.

After the wars (post-1815) abolitionists waited to see the consequences of abolition. In the early 1820s the abolitionists turned their attention to ending slavery itself. The critical questions were, should emancipation be immediate or gradual, and should compensation be made? Again, women were at the forefront of the abolitionist campaign (a campaign which dovetailed with the wider drive for reform, notably for parliamentary reform). But it was also aided by the powerful voice of black Christianity echoing from the new congregations in the Caribbean. And when Parliament was finally reformed in 1832 it spelled the end of slavery; the new MPs, from the new Britain, were basically opposed to slavery.

The slaves were partly emancipated in 1834, and fully in 1838, at the cost of a massive £20 million compensation to the *planters*. The abolitionists asked why not to the slaves? There were fears throughout the islands that the 750,000 freed slaves would seek revenge on their former owners and tormentors. In the event black freedom came peacefully and the ex-slaves rejoiced, often in and around their churches and chapels. The British slave system, conceived, nurtured and secured in violence on an epic scale, ended peaceably. The slave owners were rewarded with a social tranquillity which their past actions had hardly deserved.

After 1838 the British abolition movement continued to thrive, buoyed along by a remarkably self-righteous sense of its own moral rectitude. This was a powerful ingredient in the cultural imperialism which became integral to British dealings with peoples the world over throughout the nineteenth century. British anti-slavery was directed at societies where slavery persisted: in Africa, in India – and in the Americas. The British also continued to campaign against the persisting slave trade, across the Atlantic and Indian oceans, using the Royal Navy and regular treaties with slave trading nations (notably in Africa). The British waged a global war against slave trading, always keen to broadcast their national abolitionist virtue. In the process, however, the abolitionist movement served to erect an impressive smoke-screen between its own actions and the history of earlier British slave trading. This has also influenced modern historians. Too often, there has been a tendency to laud British abolition to the exclusion of British slave trading. After all, in the century before the British ended the slave trade, they had transported almost 3 million Africans across the Atlantic.

The ending of British colonial slavery left other slave systems intact. North America was the most obvious of thriving slave systems in the Americas, its cotton industry powered by enforced internal black migrations. It was a slave trade which, though lacking the physical horrors of the ocean crossing, had traumas of its own, notably the separation of families. Like the British system, North American slavery showed no signs of collapsing of its own accord – thanks to cotton. There was of course a growing American anti-slavery sentiment, especially in the North. But the culture of the South was so wedded to slavery, and to the racist culture which it spawned, that black freedom seemed as far away as ever. The South entered a *laager* mentality, besieged by critics (and a hostile industrial system) in the North and by the descant of international abolitionist criticism led by the British. The South evolved a way of life, a culture, which seemed in a time-warp and the centre of which was slavery. Slave owners turned their back on the modernising ideas of democracy (forged in 1776 and 1789), and on the progress of industrial change, insisting instead on an attachment to a slave-owning world which had rapidly collapsed elsewhere.

The English-speaking world had forged ahead with its collective attachment to broadly based freedoms; of industrial progress, political change, the freedom to invest and to labour. But slavery in the American South was resistant to all this and more. It also attracted a growing sense of moral and religious outrage among outsiders who thought slavery utterly at odds with their ideals. Abolition in the North became a crusade, influenced and shaped at many critical junctures by the example and help of British abolition. Again, women were the leaders of the campaign. It has been described as a 'transatlantic sisterhood'. There was a movement of abolitionists – men and women, black and white – back and forth across the Atlantic, drumming up agitation against slavery in the US South. The real strength of American abolition was local. But it faced an ever more resistant Southern slave system, always keen to point to Haiti (or to the declining fortunes of the West Indian islands) to show what black freedom would bring. Economic self-interest, racism and selective biblical exegesis blended into a powerful and resistant pro-slavery argument which lapped back and forth throughout the American South. The slave lobby claimed that Southern slaves were often better off than other free peoples: Irish labourers, freed slaves in the West Indies and Haiti, factory workers in Britain.

Ending Southern slavery would involve much more than black freedom. It would bring to an end Southern society itself. At this point we enter the debate about slavery and the American Civil War. To maintain their way of life – at the heart of which was slavery – Southerners were prepared to leave the Union, and to fight. Though slavery did not *cause* that war, the war ensured that slavery would be brought to an end. Slavery gave the North the opportunity to rally support and to claim the moral high ground. Thus, American slavery ended in the bloodshed of the Civil War, with Southern slaves drifting away from their owners and plantations whenever the war came close, securing their own freedom or joining the Union forces. In January 1863 Lincoln issued the Emancipation Proclamation. In 1865 the Thirteenth Amendment confirmed black freedom across the USA.

Black freedom in the United States left other slave systems exposed, notably in Brazil and Cuba. In both countries, shifts in the local economies, particularly the development of the new tobacco and coffee industries, keen to secure cheap labour, served to revive slavery. A number of slave traders still found it worthwhile to run the gauntlet of the British and American navies to deposit African slaves in Cuba and Brazil. In fifty years, for example, the Royal Navy seized some 1,600 vessels, and 150,000 Africans. Even so, an estimated 2,737,900 slaves were shipped from Africa to the Americas between 1810 and 1867 (years when abolition was supposedly in force). By the late 1860s the Atlantic trade had been brought to an end, though throughout the nineteenth century the flow of African slaves continued eastward, across the Indian Ocean.

Black slavery proved most durable in Cuba and Brazil, though in both places it came under increasing attack from local and international opponents. Cuba held on to its slaves until 1886. Brazil was even more tenacious. Brazilian slave owners derived most of their nineteenth-century slaves, like the Americans, from an internal slave trade. Though slaves were important on the plantations, especially the coffee plantations, they were of decreasing importance within the broader labouring force. By the 1880s slaves were simply quitting the plantations, and violence against slave owners increased. The Brazilian slave system was collapsing by the time it was abolished in May 1888.

The final death of slavery in the Americas did not mean the end of slavery itself. Indeed the Anti-Slavery Society, formed to attack British slavery in the early nineteenth century, continues to this day, in the form of Slavery International. The British, in their global conquests and expansion in the nineteenth century, discovered that slavery took many forms, and was not as easily curbed or outlawed as they imagined. Across the world, the British brought to their dealings with indigenous societies a determination to stamp out local variants of slavery. Yet here was a remarkable volte face. The people who had perfected the Atlantic slave trade, who had secured enormous economic advantage from slavery in their American colonies, had become, in a very short period, the most aggressively abolitionist people on earth. What had happened?

93

It took a mere fifty years (1787–1838) for the British to end their own slave system. By the time slaves were freed throughout the British West Indies, Britain had changed dramatically. It was emerging as an urbanised, industrialising society with different economic outlooks from those which had shaped and nurtured slavery. The history of British Atlantic slavery was thoroughly capitalist from the first. Metropolitan backers and merchants, with government support, invested in speculative colonial settlements using African slave labour. And the whole slave system emerged to the economic benefit of British financial and commercial interests. Of course it was quite different from the industrial capitalism which developed in the nineteenth century. But there was little doubt that colonial slavery was a critical form of investment and accumulation for British finance. And of all the curiosities in the history of slavery, few remain more troublesome for historians than the way it was ended.

There is no reason to doubt that the British continued to view slavery as profitable at the moment it came under attack after 1787. The initial abolitionist assaults did not emphasise slavery's unprofitability. Their prime objections were moral and religious. Yet from the early days, abolitionists sought to suggest an alternative economic scheme of things; a way of trading to and from Africa which would maintain British interests, without resorting to slavery. The Quakers, Thomas Clarkson and Equaino were among the first to suggest that Africa offered a plentiful market for British goods, and could be a source of untold natural resources. Open, free trade to and from Africa could become as important as the slave trade itself. Thus the foundations were laid for an economic reappraisal of the slaving system. That reappraisal became ever more pronounced in the 1820s and 1830s. Even the female-led boycott of sugar suggested that domestic social habits need not necessarily rely on the fruits of slave labour.

By 1789 abolitionists had drafted an alternative to slavery. But their *political* progress was held up by the upheavals of the French Revolution. Even then, there were long-term gains for the abolitonist cause, notably following the disasters in and around Haiti, and the growing weariness about the cost of maintaining so volatile and complex a system as African slavery in the colonies. All this took place in a British society slowly shifting, at critical points, towards a more refined sensibility. Concerns about violence, about punishments, about maltreatment (of the mad, of the criminal, of animals – and of slaves) all served to blend into a generalised but influential feeling that society needed to change. This seemed glaringly obvious in the case of the slave colonies. If slavery could only be maintained by repeated acts of individual and communal violence against the slaves, and if slaves could only show their true feelings by a persistent rumble of discontent, and by occasional acts of violent desperation, the question of whether it was worthwhile continued to be asked.

Ultimately the British resolved that it was not. More importantly perhaps, they had also found other forms of economic activity which seemed both profitable and morally neutral. By the 1820s it was more attractive to urge the British people to consume tropical produce grown *outside* the British slave system (even though some of it was produced by other countries' slaves). By then, a familiar

British pattern had once again become noticeable. Economic self-interest (a growing attachment to free trade) was proving a comfortable bedfellow to a new form of morality (anti-slavery). Even so, the British were inconsistent. When ex-slaves fled the West Indian plantations, they were often replaced by armies of Indian indentured labourers ('coolies') transported from India in conditions which were uncomfortably reminiscent of the slave trade. Those Indians were then tied to the land, usually for seven years. This indenture system lasted well into the twentieth century, and saw millions of Indians shipped to all corners of the British tropical empire (the West Indies, East and South Africa and the South Pacific) to undertake slave-like work under British supervision. Yet these were the years during which British anti-slavery trumpeted its moral superiority around the world.

Perhaps the most important claim of the abolition movement on behalf of the slave was the simple question: 'Am I not a man and a brother?' The simplicity of that assertion disguises a fundamental issue. Atlantic slavery had hinged on the *denial* of this claim. The Atlantic slave trade was the beginning of a process which denied humanity to its millions of victims. The legacy of the slave trade was at its most striking in the peopling of the Americas. Until the 1820s as we have seen the majority of people who had crossed the Atlantic to live in the Americas were African. Those Africans entered an Atlantic slave economy which was structured by social and racial groupings. The Atlantic slave trade thus served to racialise society, and this had profound consequences on both sides of the Atlantic. Of course there was a complex cultural history of white attitudes towards black humanity, which can be seen in classical and biblical texts and which pre-dated the settlements in the Americas. But at the height of Atlantic slavery it was *assumed* that to be black was to be a slave. This had not always been the case. In the pioneering days of American settlement, the links between blackness and slavery were much less clear. The emergence of the plantation complex, peopled by ever more Africans from the slave ships, ensured that the formula changed. To be black was to be a slave. And a black slave was denied crucial areas of humanity both by local and metropolitan law, and at the hands of slave owners and planters everywhere.

The slave became a non-person: a chattel, a thing, an object to be bequeathed and inherited, sold and bought. Moreover the slave was black; a person transmuted into a object of loathing by white society. All slave societies devised complex legal and social conventions for maintaining the separation, the uniqueness of blacks, by limiting their access to the law, to property, to certain relationships with white people. At times, whites went to bizarre lengths to maintain these racial hierarchies (and to ensure that whites remained on top). The end results were legal codes and local conventions which secured black humanity a permanent and inherited place at the bottom of the social heap. Nor was this simply a matter of legal practice. Whites everywhere across the Americas *internalised* this hierarchy, believing in and living out as daily reality the racialism of slavery. Thus were sown the seeds of a racism which, though planted in the peculiarities of slave society, were to bear fruit long after slavery had collapsed.

Even the oft-repeated abolitionist phrase, 'Am I not a man and a brother?' failed to dislodge the widespread allegiance to this racialised view of mankind. In the short term, however, the millions of ex-slaves who secured their freedom in the Americas in the nineteenth century were heirs to an intellectual and political worldview which consigned them, at best, to the bottom of local society; at worst, it cast them beyond the pale of humanity completely. It was a process made worse, in the course of the nineteenth and twentieth centuries, by the emergence of new social and natural sciences which devised racial categories of mankind to the great disadvantage of blacks everywhere.

By the late 1860s the Atlantic slave trade had been brought to an end. By then, slavery was extinct in all the old slave societies save Cuba and Brazil (where the systems were tottering but staggered on for another twenty years). Slaves everywhere rejoiced at their moment of personal or collective emancipation. But freedom was to bring problems of its own. Despite those difficulties (of racism, continued exploitation and economic marginality), there was no turning back. Former slave holders were often heard to mutter that they knew of ex-slaves who yearned for the old days. The ex-slaves told a different tale.

Conclusion

Historians are generally agreed that the Atlantic slave trade was a critical force in the shaping of the modern western world. Nor is this simply a matter of numbers – of the massive enforced movements of peoples across the Atlantic. The consequences of those transportations are so varied and so profound that historians are often bewildered about how best to describe their historical significance.

The slave trade had fundamental consequences for three continents. It helped to populate the Americas with African peoples, whose removal had profound consequences for their varied African homelands. The labours of African slaves (and of their locally born descendants) converted key areas of the Americas to profitable cultivation. The profits and material well-being which flowed from those labours – mainly on plantations – benefited the colonial and metropolitan backers of colonial slavery. But those benefits went much further than the tight circle of immediate commercial and financial interests. Indeed, the fruits of slave labour served to transform social life on both sides of the Atlantic, and later the whole world. The taste for slave-grown products became basic to western life. The taste for tobacco, for sugar and for all things sweetened stemmed directly from the slave quarters of the Americas.

Societies across the Americas became addicted to slave labour. Slavery in effect became a culture in itself, not simply among the slaves who were forced to re-create their personal and communal lives in their American exile, but also among their owners. Slave owners found it hard or impossible to contemplate life without slavery. Slaves provided the basis of their prosperity and also formed the very basis of society at large. It shaped a culture for both blacks and whites. In the process there emerged complex ideologies justifying the relegation of humanity to the level of property, the reduction of black people to chattels. It necessarily spawned ideas – and social systems – which were racially determined.

Slavery was thus the critical force in the racialising of the western world in the years after the European invasions of the Americas. The legacy of those ideas lived on – and continues – long after slavery in the Americas itself had ended. Hence what seems at first glance to be a relatively simple historical story – the slave trade – forms the core of a complex historical process whose ramifications continue to reverberate throughout the modern world. Historians continue to probe the fine details of slavery and the slave trade. But we know enough already to assert that here was one of the most significant historical forces in the shaping of the Atlantic world.

Further Reading

For a recent comprehensive account of slavery in its wider setting, see Robin Blackburn, *The Making of New World Slavery. From the Baroque to the Modern, 1492–1800*, London, 1997. The Brazilian story is best approached through Stuart Schwartz, *Sugar Plantations in the Formation of Brazilian Society, Bahia, 1550–1835*, Cambridge, 1985. The early history of slavery in North America is described in Ira Berlin, *Many Thousands Gone. The First Two Centuries of Slavery in North America*, Cambridge, MA., 1998, but see also Robert William Fogel, *Without Consent of Contract. The Rise and Fall of American Slavery*, New York, 1989.

Two books provide broad surveys of the history of slavery: Peter Kolchin, *American Slavery*, London, 1995, and James Walvin, *Black Ivory, A History of British Slavery*, London, 1992. Hugh Thomas, *The Slave Trade*, London, 1997, is especially good on the

Iberian involvement with slavery.

Specific aspects of the history of the slave trade and slavery can be found in two excellent encyclopedias: Paul Finkelman and Joseph C. Miller, (eds), *Macmillan Encyclopedia of World Slavery*, (2 vols), New York, 1998, and Seymour Drescher and Stanley L. Engerman (eds), *A Historical Guide to World Slavery*, Oxford, 1998.

For those interested in Africa, a good starting point is John Illife, *Africans. The History of a Continent*, Cambridge, 1995, and John Thornton, *Africa and Africans in the Making of the Atlantic World, 1400–1680*, Cambridge, 1992.

Anyone interested in locating the history of slavery in its imperial setting should consult the excellent essays in Nicholas Canny (ed.), *The Oxford History of the British Empire*, vol. 1, *Origins*, and P.J. Marshall (ed.), Vol. 2, *The Eighteenth Century*, Oxford, 1998. The decline of slavery is admirably described in Robin Blackburn, *The Overthrow of Colonial Slavery, 1776–1848*, London, 1988.

Index

abolition
  early attitudes 23–4, 56–7
  ending of slave trade 74–85
  ending of slavery 85–97, 100–1
  illegal trade after abolition
    33
Africa
  African middlemen 29–31,
    32, 35
  internal slavery 31, 88
  slave trade 23–46
alcohol 30
America (colonies/USA)
  Civil War and abolition
    88–91
  independence 49, 76–7
  internal slave trade 55–6, 78
  see also Chesapeake; plantations
Amsterdam 24
Angola 7
Azores 2, 3

Bahia 34
'Baptist War' 68

Barbados 13–14, 16, 18–19,
    48–9, 68, 75
Bath 54
Benin, Bight of 28
Bermuda 13
Biafra, Bight of 28
Brazil 4–6, 7, 10–13 passim, 18,
    33, 34, 48, 55–6
  end of slavery 91–3, 100
Bristol 16, 24, 26–7, 54

Canaries 3
Cape Verde islands 3
Caribbean – see West Indies
Cartagena 9
Charleston 51, 54
Chesapeake/Virginia 15–16,
    22, 50, 53, 54, 68
children 36
  see also families
Christian church 4, 8, 66,
    67–8, 86–7
  see also Quakers
Clarkson, Thomas 79–80, 82, 95

cocoa 16

coffee 16, 54, 58, 92

Columbus, Christopher 5

cotton 13, 16, 55, 56–7, 88–9

Cuba 8, 9, 33, 91–2, 100

culture
  culture based on slavery – *see* racism
  slave culture xiv, 43–4, 52–3, 64–70

deaths
  executions 61
  in transit xii–xiii, 36–8

Demerara 68

Denmark 85

descendants of slaves x, xii
  see also racism

disease/sickness
  Europeans in Africa 7, 35
  slaves xiv, 5, 45–6, 63–4

Dutch – *see* Netherlands

Dutch West Indian Company 10–11

Egypt, ancient ix

Elmina 10–11

environment 49

Equiano, Olaudah 80, 95

Europe x–xi, xii, xiii, 19–20

families 55–6, 64, 68–9

firearms 29, 30, 57

Fox, George 76

French Revolution 82–3, 95

Gambia 26

Georgia 22

gold 1

Gold Coast 26, 28

Great Britain
  and abolition 76, 78–82, 84–5, 87–8, 93–7
  economy 57–9
  and slave trade 10, 12–22, 23–8, 35

Greece, ancient ix

Haiti/St Domingue 8, 60, 71, 75, 82–4, 90

Hawkins, Sir John 10

houses 49, 54, 57

Igbo peoples 28, 65

indenture system 13, 74, 97

India ix, 57, 88, 92, 97

Indians xv, 4–5, 8, 15, 34, 48, 74, 97
indigo 16

Jamaica 8, 14–15, 19, 49, 61, 68
Jamestown 15

language 52–3, 65–6
Lima 9
Lincoln, Abraham 91
Liverpool 16, 24, 26–7
London 16, 21, 24, 27
Luanda 7

Madeira 2, 3
male/female ratios 31, 36
Maryland – see Chesapeake
Mediterranean ix, 1, 2
metalware 57
Mexico City 9
music 66–7
Muslims 1, 3

Navigation Acts 21–2
Nelson, Lord 22
Netherlands/Dutch 6, 10–12, 13, 18–19, 20, 26
New England 20

numbers of slaves xi–xii, 6–7, 25, 26, 32–3, 56

Pernambuco 13
Philadelphia 76
plantations 13, 14–16, 47–60
Portugal/ Portuguese 1–11 passim, 17–20 passim, 25–6, 48
Principe 3
privateers 10

Quakers 76, 79, 81, 95

racism xv–xvi, 17–18, 48, 59, 97–100, 103–4
religion 4, 8, 67–8, 86–7
resistance 40, 60–61, 68, 71, 86
    Haiti revolt 82–4
rewards/incentives 64, 71
rice 50, 51–2, 54, 58
Roman empire ix
Royal African Company 13–14, 23
Royal Navy 22, 88, 92
rum 58

Saharan trade routes ix, 1

St Domingue – *see* Haiti
São Tome 2, 3
Savanna 54
scholarship x–xi, xvii
selling of slaves 42, 55–6, 78
Senegambia 27–8
shipping 21–2
  slave ships xii, xiv, 32–41,
    81–2
Sierra Leone 26, 27–8
skilled slaves 50–1, 70
Slavery International 93
Smith, Adam: *The Wealth of
    Nations* 77
South Carolina 22, 50, 51, 68
Spain 1, 3, 5, 7–9, 10, 12, 14,
    19–20, 48
sugar 2–3, 5–7, 12, 18–19, 95,
    103
  see also plantations

textiles 30, 57, 78
Thirteenth Amendment 91

Thirty Years War 12
tobacco 12, 13, 15–16, 21, 52,
    54, 58, 92, 103
'triangular trade' xi, 48
Turner, Nat 68

USA – *see* America

Vera Cruz 9
Vesey, Denmark 68
violence 61–3, 70–3
Virginia see
    Chesapeake/Virginia

West Africa 25–6, 27–8
West Indies/Caribbean 5, 7,
    20–2, 26, 33, 48–54 *passim,*
    58, 79, 85
  see also Barbados; Haiti;
    Jamaica
Wilberforce, William 82
women abolitionists 81, 90,
    95